Rights to Light

RIGHTS TO LIGHT

Patrick J. C. Ellis B.SC. ARICS

1989

THE ESTATES GAZETTE LIMITED
151 WARDOUR STREET, LONDON W1V 4BN

First published 1989
ISBN 0 7282 0131 3

*This book was commissioned
and produced for the Estates Gazette Limited
by Leaf Coppin Publishing Ltd*

Photoset by Input Typesetting Ltd, London
Printed by Hobbs the Printers Ltd, Southampton SO9 2UZ

CONTENTS

	Table of Cases	vii
1	Why the Right to Light is Important	1
2	What is the Right to Light?	5
3	Where the Right to Light may be a Problem	12
4	How Light is defined and measured	20
5	The Cases which come to Law	28
6	How Disputes are decided	38
7	Is it worth it?	45
8	Planning for Light	50
	Bibliography	55
	Index	56

TABLE OF CASES

Allen and Another v
 Greenwood and Another
 [1975] 1 ALL ER
 819   6,35–6
Andrews v Waite [1907] 2 Ch
 500   33
Carr Saunders v Dick McNeil
 Associates Ltd and Others
 [1986] 1 WLR 922   37, 43
Colls v Home & Colonial
 Stores [1904] AC 179   4, 9,
 10, 29, 31–2, 34
Ecclesiastical Commissioners
 for England v Kino [1880]
 14 ChD 213   40
Fishenden v Higgs and Hill Ltd
 [1935] 153 LT 128   33
Gamble v Doyle (1971) 219 EG
 310   34
Hawker v Tomalin [1969] 20
 P & CR 550   10
Hawkins v Rutter [1892] 1 QB
 668   5
Leeds Industrial Co-Operative
 Society Ltd v Slack [1924]
 AC 851   45
Lyme Valley Squash Club Ltd
 v Newcastle under Lyme
 Borough Council and
 Another [1985] 2 All ER
 405   28–9
Mathias v Davies (1970) 214
 EG 1111   29
Metaxides v Adamson (1971)
 219 EG 935   35

Moore v Hall (1878) 3 QBD
 178   6, 43
Newham and Others v Lawson
 and Others [1971] 22 P & CR
 852   35
News of the World Ltd v Allen
 Fairhead & Sons Ltd [1931]
 2 Ch 402   32–3
Ough v King [1967] 3 All ER
 859   34
Presland v Bingham [1889]
 ChD 268   40–1
Price v Hilditch [1930] 1 Ch
 500   5, 37, 43
Pugh and Another v Howels
 and Another [1984] 48 P &
 CR 298   36–7
Scott v Pape (1886) 31 ChD
 554   6, 30
Sheffield Masonic Hall Co. v
 Sheffield Corporation
 [1932] 2 Ch 17   43
Shelfer v City of London
 Electric Lighting Co. [1895]
 1 Ch 287   31
Tapling v Jones (1865) 20 CB
 (NS) 166   33, 40
Wheaton v Maple [1890] 3 Ch
 48   10
Wheeldon v Burrows [1879] 12
 ChD 31   28
William Cory & Son Limited v
 City of London Real
 Property Company Limited
 (1954) 163 EG 514   10,
 33–4

I WHY THE RIGHT TO LIGHT IS IMPORTANT

Introduction

The right to light is a subject understood by very few, yet many property owners (householders and developers) could be concerned by it at least once in their lifetime. As land in city centres becomes more valuable and demand for space increases, so developers want to build larger blocks with a greater density. Inevitably, this means building out closer to neighbouring buildings or increasing the height, and, more often than not, both. Developers have found to their cost that the owners of the block next door have taken exception to such schemes and years of planning have been brought to a halt; it is, quite literally, 'back to the drawing board'. Nor is the problem confined to the commercial sector. One of the most frequent objections to a planning proposal in a residential area is the effect on the light – 'my kitchen will be plunged into darkness,' 'the garden will hardly get the sun any more' and similar complaints.

Why does this happen and what can be done to remedy the situation? The answer to the first question rests generally, as with so many matters that have a legal origin, in a lack of understanding. Ignorance of the law is no excuse. The remedy will depend on which side of the fence the party finds himself. Every case is different and the outcome will differ accordingly. This book should give an understanding of the factors that are taken into account and, dare I say it, throw some light on the subject. But first a word of caution: if in doubt anyone involved in a dispute concerning the right to light should consult an expert (reading this book is not sufficient!). This can save a lot of unnecessary heartache.

It was not until the early Georgian period that the importance of natural light within buildings began to be appreciated and to be reflected generally in architectural terms. The frequency and size of window openings, particularly the height, enabled a large amount of natural light to enter rooms and penetrate to a great depth. Once a standard had been established it became necessary to protect it. 'Ancient lights' developed in a legal sense and cases became more common as disputes arose. The Prescription Act 1832 was an attempt to rationalise the extent and acquisition of easements, including light. The current law relating to the right to light is based on these nineteenth-century foundations (see further below, p. 8).

The introduction of greater control over the construction of buildings themselves and, later, the town and country planning system, laid down standards to be followed in terms not only of natural light within buildings but also of space in between to ensure that this would be maintained. Before the evolution of the modern planning process, the right to light was important as it was one of the few practical methods of governing reasonable development. On the one hand, if it was not possible for the freeholder to acquire any rights he would have no protection against new developments being erected that virtually obliterated the daylight from his property unless he owned extensive land around the building. On the other hand, if he had a right to light there needed to be a limitation on its extent since, if there were an absolute right to light, then whoever built first could have prevented any construction which diminished the light to the building, however minimally.

The planning process is not, however, a substitute for rights to light. The planning process certainly includes standards for daylighting, sunlighting and space between buildings, but these are guide-lines to be considered along with many other factors. Invariably, these other factors (often economic or political) are the deciding ones as to whether a particular application is successful and they can vary from one side of a street to the other, particularly, for example, if the local authority boundary runs down the middle.

Yet, and this cannot be too strongly emphasised, the factors that govern the right to light are different from those taken into account during the planning process. The granting of planning permission does not affect an owner's right to light. A successful planning application does not mean that the proposed development is therefore satisfactory in terms of daylighting to the neighbouring buildings. Conversely, a right to light does

Set-backs in a light-well. The varying slopes probably reflect certain defined angles within which building is permitted

not have to be proved to be able to oppose successfully a planning application for development on neighbouring land.

Whilst it is true to say that the importance attached to light will inevitably differ according to whether, for instance, it is a house in the country or a house in a city centre that is in question, the right to light is, broadly speaking, one which could be acquired by any piece of land with respect to another piece of land. It is fundamental to our legal system that the rights of an individual are maintained and upheld. The Earl of Halsbury LC in a leading case (*Colls v Home & Colonial Stores*, see below, p. 31) said, 'Light, like air, is the common property of all . . . it is the common right of all to enjoy it, but it is the exclusive property of none.' The right to light is an unusual one in our legal system: something can be done on a neighbour's land which, after a period of time, can impose severe restrictions on the possibilities of developing one's own land. In the same situation, however, one could also impose severe limitations on a neighbour's ability to develop (on his) land. In other words the right can belong to both parties. To understand why this is the case, an appreciation of the general legal position and the practicalities of how this affects everyone is required. Accordingly, in the remainder of the book consideration will be given to legal aspects such as the easement of light itself, the key cases and the arguments used. On the practical side, there will be an assessment of the situations where the different parties (developer, neighbour, designer, solicitor, surveyor) may encounter a rights to light problem, a discussion of the relationship between rights to light and planning, and a brief examination of how light is measured and how it is valued.

2 WHAT IS THE RIGHT TO LIGHT?

The Easement of Light

What is the right to light? It is not an automatic, natural right enjoyed by all landowners: it is a specific right which an individual landowner may acquire over the land of a neighbour. It is one of a species of legal property rights known as an easement. An easement is a right attaching to, and benefiting, one piece of land, and exercisable over someone else's land. Put technically, there must be a dominant piece of land in favour of which the easement is claimed, and a servient piece of land over which that easement is exercised (Lord Coleridge CJ in *Hawkins v Rutter* [1892] 1 QB 668). It is, thus, a right over, or a restriction upon, one piece of land for the benefit of another. In the specific context of an easement of light, the servient land is that owned by the developer or other person erecting a building, and the dominant land is that owned by a neighbour who finds that the light flowing to his property is being obstructed by those works.

The easement of light is a negative easement. That is to say, it is a restriction rather than a positive right (like a right of way) but, once it has been acquired or obtained, no positive action is required to maintain it except, of course, to protect it from someone else's infringing or taking it away. There are, however, certain conditions which have to be met. The right claimed must demonstrate the characteristics demanded by the law of an easement, and must have been acquired in one of the recognised ways.

In broad terms certain characteristics have been established: the right does not relate to an individual, but rather it relates to the access and use of light over the servient tenement for certain windows or lights in the dominant tenement (*Price v Hilditch* [1930] 1 Ch 500). A building can even be vacant so long as a potential user exists (*Moore v Hall* (1878) 3 QBD 178) and so long as the right has not been abandoned completely.

Whilst the right attaches to the land there must be an actual building with clearly defined apertures through which the light can pass. There is no right to light to a field or garden, for example, and likewise none to a blank wall. The exception to this is where a building has been demolished and is about to be rebuilt. In such an instance it is possible to transfer the rights previously enjoyed, through the windows of the former building to the new one (*Scott v Pape* (1886) 31 ChD 554). There is no right to a view nor to reflected light, because of the uncertainty and subjective nature of the items in question. It has for many years been considered by the same token that there is no right to sunlight. One case has cast doubt on this assumption, though there are reasons to believe this may have been an exceptional decision (*Allen v Greenwood*, see p. 35, below).

In essence, there are three ways to acquire a right to light: firstly, it can be implied; secondly, by express creation and, thirdly, by prescription. An implied right to light may arise if it can properly be inferred that there was an intention that one should be granted or reserved. A right can be expressly created by grant or reservation. An owner cannot have an easement over his own land, but if he sells that land he can place restrictions on it to benefit neighbouring land which he has retained. In practice, an expressly created easement usually takes the form of a right to light agreement. For example (see figure), the owner of land 'A' is given permission to build anything up to a maximum height of fifty feet (fifteen metres) by agreement of and notwithstanding the effect on land 'B'. Conversely, the owner of land 'C' and 'D' may sell off 'D' and reserve in an agreement the right to build to a hundred feet (thirty metres) on the retained land 'C', notwithstanding the effect on the light to land 'D'. Right to light agreements often have drawings showing agreed profiles which can be built up to on either land. The agreements are either prohibitive or permissive in nature. Prohibitive ones state a limit beyond which one owner cannot build without further agreement from the other party. Permissive ones state a limit within which an owner is at liberty to build but thereafter any building is undertaken at the owner's risk. The difference may seem a subtle one, but the former is

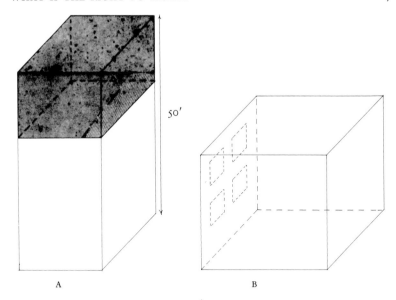

A   B

PERMISSION TO BUILD UP TO 50′ IN THE FUTURE BY AGREEMENT

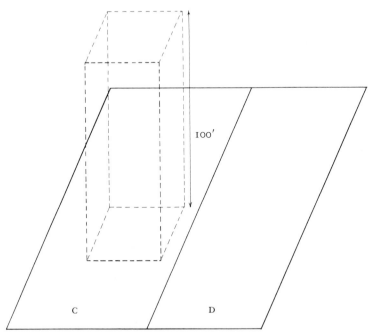

C   D

RESERVATION TO PERMIT FUTURE BUILDING ON LAND C

absolute whilst the latter may still give scope for advance in the future.

Prescription

The third, and by far the most common, way of acquiring a right to light is by prescription or long usage. In this context, the Prescription Act 1832 is key legislation. Section 3 states:

> that when the Access and Use of Light to and for any Dwelling House, Workshop or other building shall have been actually enjoyed therewith for the full period of Twenty Years without Interruption the Right thereto shall be deemed absolute and indefeasible . . . unless . . . the same was enjoyed by some Consent or Agreement expressly made . . . by Deed or Writing.

On the surface it seems straightforward enough: once a building has enjoyed light for twenty years the owner has an absolute right to the light unless there is some right to light agreement in existence.

Section 4 of the Act goes on to say that the twenty years

> shall be taken to be the Period next before some (Law) Suit or Action wherein the Claim . . . shall be brought into question and that no . . . other Matter shall be deemed to be an Interruption . . . unless the same shall have been . . . acquiesced in for One Year after the Party interrupted shall have had . . . Notice thereof . . .

Again seemingly straightforward: the owner must have had the light for the previous twenty years at least, those rights being lost, or at least modified, if his light has been obstructed for a year and he has not made a claim.

The idea behind the Prescription Act was sound but unfortunately the way it was drafted gave rise to much confusion. In common law, prior to this Act, an easement was acquired by use over a long period taken to be the period 'whereof the memory of man runneth not to the contrary'. The date 1189 was taken as the beginning of such a period and, in theory, to prove someone held a right he had to show the right had been enjoyed since that time: a right claimed by long usage was usually shown by erecting a sign stating 'Ancient Lights'. The Act made this a more manageable concept since it was only necessary to prove the enjoyment of the right over the preceding twenty years. However, it soon became clear that, by making the right 'absolute and indefeasible', the Act could cause land to be blighted since it appeared to prevent any reduction in light to the neighbouring land. The courts have grappled ever since with this question and from the ensuing case law have developed the legal precedents which now make up the right to light. A relatively short and minor statute, the Rights of Light Act, was introduced in 1959 but did not alter the overall principles outlined here. On the details of this legislation, see below, p. 42.

It was not until a case in the early part of this century that some certainty on the subject of an 'absolute and indefeasible' right to light was established. *Colls v Home & Colonial Stores* [1904] AC 179 concerned a new building in central London and its effect on a building on the opposite side of the road. The new building did give rise to a loss of light to the neighbouring building but mainly owing to the deep plan layout of this building which only had windows facing out on to the street. Joyce J in the lower court ruled against an injunction, the Court of Appeal ordered partial demolition and the House of Lords found on the basis of the original judgment of Joyce J. Lord Davey, commenting on section 3 of the Act, explained the effect of the provision. It was not to alter the nature of the pre-existing law as to the nature and extent of the right, but merely to alter the conditions or length of user by which the right might be acquired. Lord Lindley stated that:

> An owner of ancient lights is entitled to sufficient light according to the ordinary notions of mankind for the comfortable use and enjoyment of his house . . . if it is a dwelling house or for the beneficial use and occupation of . . . a warehouse, a shop or other place of business.

He went on to make an observation that is widely endorsed by practitioners in the subject today, namely, that the right to light is a peculiar kind of easement.

Actionable Interference

What has since been held to be sufficient light for the ordinary notions of mankind is discussed later (see below, p. 25), but *Colls* laid down the principle that the right to light is a right to a sufficient quantum of light for certain purposes. Whether the right has been materially affected is assessed on the basis not of how much has been taken away but rather of how much is left. An obstruction of the right to light is commonly regarded, therefore, as a nuisance and not a trespass. It is thus possible for a developer to obstruct his neighbour's light providing he leaves him with sufficient light. 'It is always to be remembered that there is no property in light and that the question in light action is always not how much the Plaintiff has lost but how much he will retain if the Defendant's building is erected. If adequate light be left the Plaintiff has no right to complain' (*Hawker v Tomalin* [1969] 20 P & CR 550).

It is the question of what is an 'actionable injury', and its resolution, which is usually at the centre of rights to light disputes. Upjohn J in *William Cory & Son Limited v City of London Real Property Company Limited* (see below p. 33) expressed the opinion, which is generally accepted by practitioners, that a room still has sufficient light if half the floor area of the room measured at work-top height has, on an overcast day in February, not less than 1 foot candle (see below, pp. 20–7, on measurement of light). This is commonly referred to as the '50/50' rule, and the line at the halfway position is the grumble line.

If a case can be proved and there is an actionable injury to the right of the dominant tenement, then there are two courses of action. Either the obstruction should be removed or damages in lieu should be paid to the injured party.

The Crown

One other important aspect of the Prescription Act concerns the immunity of the Crown. A right to light cannot be acquired over land belonging to the Crown or leased to a tenant of the Crown (*Wheaton v Maple* [1890] 3 Ch 48). Section 3 makes no reference to the Crown and by a rule of construction no Act of Parliament binds the Crown unless the Crown is expressly mentioned, or unless the intention to bind is clear and unmistakable. It is a remote possibility that a lost modern grant could be claimed (see below, p. 41).

3 WHERE THE RIGHT TO LIGHT MAY BE A PROBLEM

Before looking at what light is important and how it is measured let us consider some practical situations in which one might find oneself in contact with the question of the right to light.

As a Purchaser

Problems can arise for a purchaser out of the results of the search and investigation of the title or enquiries of the vendors. There could be a series of agreements recorded in the Charges Register which concern rights to light. These have invariably arisen from disputes affecting the property in the past. It is unusual for these to be discovered on the titles of residential properties but they are fairly common in city centres, particularly on older buildings with a commercial use. If a purchaser does not plan to carry out any development work or build an extension on the land then usually these are of little consequence. However, the prudent purchaser would consult the solicitors if they have not already reported on them in a report on title. Some agreements may relate to windows on or adjacent to the boundary of the site. It is possible that the windows may be subject to a licence whereby the neighbour can build in front of them without objection or the owner has to block them up. If that is the case, the purchaser has to decide whether the consequences of either of the foregoing actions are acceptable.

There could be restrictive covenants on the title which could severely limit the use and extent to which the new owner might use the property/land in the future. It may be possible to have such conditions set aside or modified by the Lands Tribunal. It is more likely, however, that the purchaser will have to accept them or seek to reach a new agreement with the party who benefits from them.

Enquiries made by the purchaser during the contract stage may reveal an unresolved dispute with a neighbour – or planning applications. In the event of the former, if the dispute relates to something which has been constructed on the land to be purchased the purchaser should be careful. It is not unknown for a new extension to have to be demolished because of a right to light.

As a Developer

Whilst developments may be undertaken on a charitable basis, it is reasonable to assume that the overriding factor for a developer is to make a profit. The developer will be aware of the need to investigate closely and assess anything which prevents or imposes a large risk on this happening. The importance to the developer of existing agreements which bind future use of a site cannot be over-stressed. If it is not practical to develop within the existing limitations he (or she) will have to establish with whom to renegotiate the agreements. The timing of any approach will be a key factor. The planning process can be slow in some parts of the country and it is unlikely that a profit margin can be sustained if failure to reach a revised agreement requires the design to be modified and a new planning permission sought.

If, however, there are no onerous points arising from the title, then the developer's concern will be confined to the design. He will be wanting to maximise the size of the development whilst at the same time maintaining or creating the right environment within the development itself. New buildings need natural light and some form of outlook, and without these the space within is rarely acceptable. Large buildings are often set back at the upper levels not in response to neighbouring buildings but rather to allow better angles of natural light to enter the new building. Atria maintain all the benefits of natural light without the problems of rain, leaves and pigeons, which call for endless maintenance in the light-wells of Victorian office and tenement blocks.

In maximising the size of the development the developer will have to take into account the maintenance of natural light to neighbouring properties. Too often, in the search for the extra floor or larger room size, the resultant proposal goes beyond

White glazed brickwork in light-wells

Set-backs on a street frontage. This may simply be a planning requirement to reduce the apparent mass from street level

the limits of acceptability to neighbours. The developer needs to be aware of and understand this problem at the earliest stage so that any modifications to the proposed structure can be made on the drawing board and any negotiations that have to take place to reach agreements to ensure the preferred scheme is built are accomplished without delay.

In this context, it is interesting to note that there is no obligation on a developer to inform neighbouring owners that the proposed development will infringe their right to light. Since the vast majority of potential rights to light claims are never made, this may explain why many developers pay the question little heed. A developer may continue to be lucky and carry on in blissful ignorance. If he is building in the middle of the Yorkshire Moors or taking away the countryside for an industrial estate or shopping centre, he will probably remain ignorant. Building in a town centre, he will have rather more chance of encountering the problem.

As a Designer

The architect or building surveyor starts with a difficult brief. The developer wants the biggest tallest widest building possible – or so it may seem. The designer has to meet this requirement whilst at the same time producing a scheme which will satisfy the planners, meet the various requirements of Building Regulations and other statutory controls *and* not infringe neighbouring rights to light. Inevitably, this is not always possible. The designer needs to inform the client at an early design stage if it is impossible to alter the envelope of a building without affecting the provision of natural light to neighbouring properties because the proposed building would alter the angles of light coming across the site. The designer should have an understanding of what may constitute a problem and, if he does not feel confident to advise further, should recommend to his client that he appoints a specialist.

The good designer will study the site and note windows in surrounding properties which could cause a problem. He will ascertain if there are any legal agreements such as restrictive covenants. If necessary, he can prepare alternative schemes for the client, one respecting agreements and the existing light angles to surrounding buildings, another to be regarded as optimal in terms of the other criteria. The client, forewarned of the potential difficulties, can then decide which course the designer should pursue. Consideration needs to be given to the long-term implications of the design. For example, the Building Regulations limit (mainly for spread of fire purposes) the amount of glazing/openings on or adjacent to the boundary of the site. Relaxations or waivers can sometimes be obtained, but there is always the possibility that if the new windows are positioned close to the boundary the neighbour may develop and severely restrict the light through them. Both privacy and an outlook may be important for the development. These may be reduced by subsequent surrounding development but they are virtually impossible to protect at law.

Just as the preferred design solution may infringe the amenities of others, so the reverse is possible. A client will not thank the designer if the light to all the new windows is later taken away. Consideration should therefore be given by the designer and the developer to cladding materials: white glazed brickwork used to be a standard specification for light-wells between commercial buildings. It does reflect a large amount of light, and an equally light finish in sensitive areas may be the factor that persuades the neighbouring owner not to pursue a claim for loss of light. Regard should be given not only to the windows of buildings at the sides and rear of the site but also to those on the opposite side of the street. By incorporating mansards or set-backs on the upper floors, an impression can be created that the design is sympathetic to the rights of neighbouring land owners. If possible the designer should locate the plant room in a non-sensitive area. As far as the neighbour is concerned, it forms part of the overall obstruction, as does a pitched roof or even a parapet. External fire escapes may be secondary to the site but they form a fairly massive obstruction in terms of light. The designer needs constantly to put himself in the neighbour's position and amend his scheme accordingly.

As a Neighbour

In almost all residential cases the neighbour will want to obstruct development and, preferably, to prevent it altogether; at the very least he will want it modified to lessen the impact. It may also be the case that in a residential context the building of an extension, for example, can create a precedent for others to follow. A neighbour has nothing seemingly to gain but everything to lose. In a commercial situation the considerations are somewhat different: the proposed building may restrict and degrade the existing one, and a neighbouring owner could have a claim for loss of light. On the other hand, a smart new office building next door, rather than a shabby Victorian block, could actually increase the value of any neighbouring commercial property, and if the new building is two storeys higher that may open up the possibility of the older building's having additional storeys added. A neighbour should therefore think carefully about the nature of his objection before initiating it.

Invariably, the first indication of a new scheme that a neighbour will receive is the letter from the planning authority giving notice of a development on adjacent land and giving a short period of time in which to object. The neighbour might bring in a surveyor at this stage to inspect the application and report on the likely impact on the property. Alternatively, a personal inspection of the application can be undertaken. Most applications have a full set of drawings accompanying them. It is possible that the developer will send a set to interested parties if requested. The neighbour or his professional adviser will have to envisage the position and size of the proposed extension or building, and which of the windows will be affected. The title will need to be checked for any rights to light agreements which could have a bearing on the case. The proposal can then be discussed with the planning officer responsible and, if necessary, with the developer and a planning objection can be made if appropriate.

Making representations at the planning stage is almost certainly the cheapest and most straightforward way of settling light problems. If planning permission is granted then careful consideration has to be given to trying to stop or modify the development on rights to light grounds. A solicitor should be able to advise on whether the owner of a neighbouring property has any rights in the first place. The owner, for example, of a house which is less than twenty years old is unlikely to have any rights. Where there is a right to light expert, advice should be sought on the extent of any claim. If a development is prevented from proceeding and the neighbour is not successful with a claim, he may have to pay to the developer a sum to cover the costs of the delay. These can be substantial.

The leaseholder who finds that it is his landlord who is developing the neighbouring land may well discover that the lease contains provisions for the landlord so to do notwithstanding an infringement to the light. Conversely, a tenant may be required to notify the landlord of anything on neighbouring land which could affect the use and enjoyment of the demise. But a landlord needs to consider his long-term position. He might himself want to do something similar later, in which case entering into some form of reciprocal agreement to allow each party to infringe the light to the neighbouring premises would be of assistance.

One option open to a neighbour is to register a 'notional screen' for the benefit of his premises. This is described in more detail below (see p. 41): it has the effect of preventing a new development acquiring rights to light over the neighbouring land. The onus is generally on the neighbour to protect the right. If nothing is done then after a period of time the rights are invariably lost or at least modified so far as the new development is concerned.

As a Solicitor

It is unlikely that a solicitor will come across rights to light matters very frequently. Where he or she does, they will arise either from the title or, more often, from an actual dispute. Broadly speaking there are two aspects: the law relating to easements; and the extent of the loss of light and the appropriate remedy. In a large number of potential residential disputes there is not any actual material loss of light but rather there is a loss of view or outlook which is perceived as a loss of light. Seldom does a right to light dispute end up in court. Most developers, particularly those with commercial ventures, will be prepared to discuss a claim and to reach an amicable solution. This is usually best achieved by either side appointing experts who negotiate and report back. Rarely is there a failure of settlement of disputes by this procedure.

As a Surveyor

Where a surveyor is called upon to advise a client, be it developer or neighbour, he should appreciate his limitations. Advice during the planning stage can be supported by discussions with the planning officer, coupled with a knowledge of such guidelines as government leaflets on designing for sunlighting and daylighting. An inspection of the site, preferably through the windows liable to be affected, should be undertaken. What may look like a problem from the outside may disappear when it is found that the room has a skylight and three windows in the other walls, all of which help to flood the room in daylight. If in doubt the surveyor should consult an expert.

Where a new development threatens a neighbour's light, the surveyor should prepare a technical analysis indicating the extent of the problem and should if necessary draw up contingency plans. The technical information (e.g. daylight plans, sunlight plans) can be used in discussions with the planners, and in preliminary talks with neighbours. For smaller extensions, it may assist agreement if a mock up of the main part of the obstruction created by the proposed extension is actually built. This can be done with plywood on a timber or scaffold framing. The neighbour can then see the effect clearly and this should either be the end of the claim, or at least bring matters to a head. The developer is ill-advised to adopt the view that no matter what the problem, money can solve it. There are people who cannot be bought off and situations where avarice will severely curtail profit margin.

The problem in rights to light disputes is to decide what type of light is relevant, how much is required and how to measure it. If a building could be erected in two minutes it would be far simpler to assess the effects of its presence and decide if there were a case to be answered. In the absence of such a possibility and in the face of the weakness of the human memory and varying weather conditions, methods have been evolved to answer these questions.

Light (as opposed to the right to light) in buildings is usually considered in terms of daylight, sunlight and artificial light. If someone were sitting in a room with a window, the daylight reaching them would consist of three components. The first is the sky component, that is the light received directly from the sky. This will vary according to the brightness of the sky but at least the sky itself is the same everywhere. The second is the externally reflected component: this is the light received from other buildings, obstructions or external surfaces; it will vary according to their relative position (height, distance away) and the reflectiveness of the surface itself. The third is the internally reflected component: this is the light received from the other surfaces (walls, ceiling, floor) within the room in question. As with external items there will be many variables. If these three components are added together the result is the total daylight in the room.

Even without considering direct sunlight or artificial light there are therefore many variables. Nonetheless, whilst every case is taken on its merits, there has to be some uniformity or general set of rules so that comparisons can be made. To do this, the number of variable items has to be reduced and certain matters have to be treated as constant. Ideally, in a rights to light issue, the only variable would be that of the building causing the obstruction in its existing and/or proposed state.

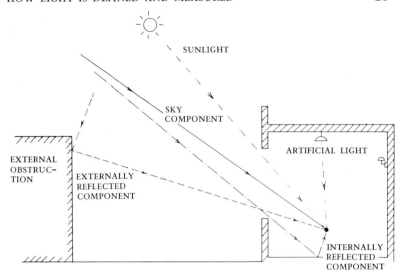

Light in a room

In order to approximate to this ideal state, the following system of assessing the light received is used.

The Sky Component

The brightness of the sky varies. In response to this the International Commission on Illumination (CIE) approved a formula for a completely overcast sky which can then be considered to be of uniform brightness. This is the CIE standard overcast sky. The sky component can be measured by one of three methods, two of them produced by the Building Research Establishment: a daylight table and a set of daylight protractors. These are useful, particularly at the early design stage, to give a broad indication of the position, and are fairly straightforward to use. Allowance can be made for matters such as type of glazing and window frames. The third and more accurate, but also more time-consuming, method is the use of Waldram diagrams. These are used in rights to light disputes and are discussed further below (see p. 23).

The Externally and Internally Reflected Components

These can also be calculated and this is sometimes necessary for a designer. However it is important to note that the courts have taken the view over the years that, as there are too many variables, these should not be taken into account in a rights to light assessment. Since these components are not constant it would be inequitable to assess a long-term obstruction on the basis of factors which can vary considerably in the short term. By way of example the Building Research Establishment has published some correction factors for percentage reductions over normal single panes of clear glass when calculating daylight factors: double glazing 10 per cent, glass blocks 60 per cent, average for timber window frames, glazing bars, etc. 25 per cent. Similarly, the average reflectiveness of building materials is: white distemper on plain plaster or plasterboard 80 per cent, fletton brickwork 30 per cent, yellow London stock 25 per cent, and white glazed brickwork 75 per cent. These variations show why it is accepted practice to ignore the reflective components in rights to light disputes and instead to concentrate on the direct light from the sky.

Artificial Light

Significant advances have been made in the quality and efficiency of artificial light. Many disputes have as their origin concern that when the lights in a room are switched off the room seems very dark. In most cases this is because the occupiers have become used to the exceptionally high standard of overall lighting that modern artificially lit rooms can have. A study of the natural light often shows that it is in fact still sufficient, albeit with some re-arrangement of the furniture so that the areas for reading and close work are better positioned, to benefit from the natural light. In the early 1970s when there were widespread power cuts most people had suddenly to rely once again on natural light. It was rather a revealing experience to discover that during daylight hours it was possible still to see and work in most rooms.

Artificial light has three main functions: it enables the occupants to see more easily when moving around; it makes close-up work easier on the eyes and it enhances appearance or particular features. Artificial light is not taken into account in rights to light matters although it is an acceptable argument to say that some rooms or areas will always require artificial lighting for reasonable use irrespective of natural light (deep plan offices, for example).

Sunlight

This can be defined as radiation from the sun whether direct or reflected. Sunshine is direct rather than diffused solar radiation. Most people would prefer to have a room or an area sunlit, provided that it does not cause glare or overheating. Unfortunately, sunshine is notoriously unreliable and there are numerous variables when considering its effect on the relationship between buildings: latitude – the higher the latitude the greater the length of shadows; orientation – buildings to the south of others can cause overshadowing; time of year – the difference in altitude and the resultant length of the sun-path (low and short in winter, high and long in summer). In addition to these, there are variations owing to the amount of cloud cover and to surrounding natural features such as hills or valleys. In design terms there are certain indicators that can be used to measure the sun-path or shadow-path and ascertain the number of hours that a proposed obstruction will effectively blot out any direct sunlight that there may be. As already mentioned, sunlight is generally not taken into account in rights to light issues.

Waldram Diagrams

The measurement of the sky component is the most widely accepted and most commonly used in rights to light disputes. It is done with a Waldram diagram. From common experience it is evident that there is a wide variation in daylight between summer and winter, different times of day, north and south aspects, reflectivity factors and so on. What had to be devised was a method to measure the quantum, intensity and distribution of light so as to compare the existing easement or situation against the proposed infringement or obstruction. Percy J. Waldram produced in the 1920s a series of papers on daylight illumination in which he discussed the natural and artificial lighting of buildings and the predetermination of day-

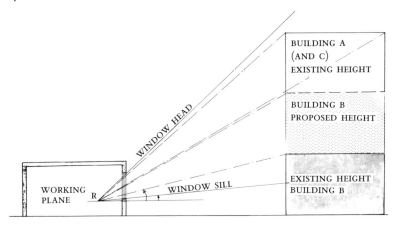

SECTION X-X

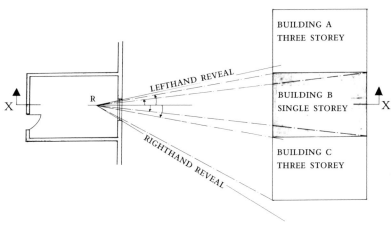

PLAN

Waldram diagrams   The buildings under study are drawn in section and plan. A position in the affected property is chosen (Point R) and sight lines are drawn which define the windows and the mass of the obstructions which can be viewed effectively from that point. These are plotted on the Waldram diagram and the area of sky visibility (i.e. the sky factor) at point R is measured in both the existing and the proposed situation. This exercise is repeated for a number of points in the affected property until a series of values measuring 0.2 per cent is plotted. These are then joined together to represent the 0.2 per cent sky factor contour. The difference between the contour for the existing situation and that for the proposed is the loss (or in some cases, the gain) arising from the proposed development.

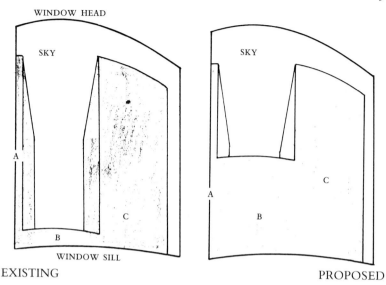

WINDOW HEAD

SKY

SKY

A

C

C

A

B

B

WINDOW SILL

EXISTING   PROPOSED

light illumination. Out of these, and discussions held between the wars, came the now generally accepted guide-lines for the measurement of rights to light. These are:

1. There is an average minimum requirement of 0.2 per cent daylight for office/clerical work and for ordinary purposes.
2. In establishing this in a room, 'sky factor' contour lines should be used.
3. Any assessment should be made at table-top or work-top height which is 850 mm or 2'9" above the floor.

By taking the uniform overcast sky, which can be considered as constant, it is possible to assess the direct light into a room (that is, the sky which is visible) before and after the proposed obstruction. Waldram diagrams are based on the concept of looking at a particular chunk of the sky, relating it to the sky as a whole and then plotting corresponding points of equal sky factor to obtain sky factor contours. The 0.2 per cent sky factor contour represents all those points having 1/500th of the light available from the whole sky. Studies have been undertaken to show that on average during the winter months there are at least 500 lumens/sq. ft. available from the whole sky. The

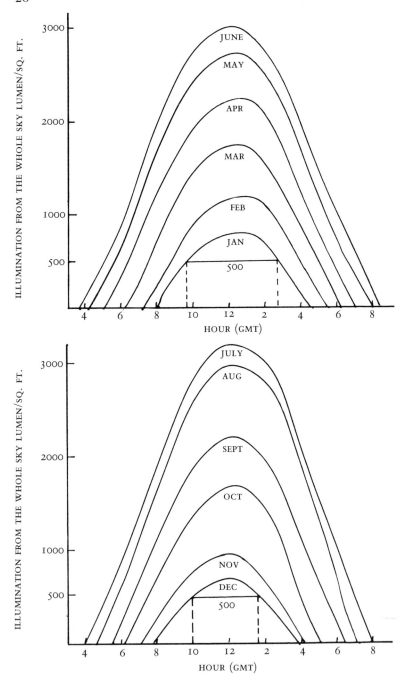

Seasonal variations in daylight (Source HMSO)

0.2 per cent contour represents the points having at least one lumen/sq. ft. (1 foot candle). This is the amount generally accepted as giving adequate light for the ordinary needs of mankind.

In virtually all cases the area nearer to the window than the 0.2 per cent contour will have a higher contour (more light) and the area further away than the 0.2 per cent contour a lower contour (less light). In practice the light from the sky in, say, the summer months is something like 3,000 lumens/sq. ft. (i.e. much brighter). But an assessment of the average state in the worst conditions (an overcast sky in winter) ensures that the adjoining resident is for the most part much better supplied with daylight.

A Waldram shows diagrammatically a picture of the view from points in a room looking out through a window. The sky factor for any point is calculated (as a combination of the amount of sky visible and the amount obstructed by, for example, buildings), and the value is noted on a plan. All those points with a sky factor of 0.2 per cent are joined together and, as a general rule, if more than half of the room has a sky factor of 0.2 per cent or more then there is adequate sky visibility (and it usually follows that there is no case to be answered – though it should be remembered that the Waldram diagrams are just part of the necessary information which is required to determine a rights to light claim).

The assessment of daylight must be treated with caution. For instance, light meters should never be used. They register so many variables such as passing clouds which the assessor is at pains to avoid. Light meters should be left to cricket umpires and photographers.

There is a natural desire to protect one's property and to maintain the general amenity and value of it. Most rights to light
disputes are settled without reference to the courts, and that
should be the aim of the professional adviser. Whilst there are
many ways of trying to classify the cases, there are, broadly
speaking, three types of dispute which get referred. The first
is where there is some form of documentation, for example a
conveyance, whereby there is either some express grant or
reservation or there is a right implied but not expressly stated.
The drafting may be vague and clarification required as to
the meaning of the document and the extent to which it is
enforceable. Two leading cases are worthy of note here to
illustrate this type of dispute.

Wheeldon v Burrows [1879] 12 ChD 31

This was a rights to light case concerning a conveyance and
the provision of windows to a shed. It was held that if an
owner of a property sells off part of that property then there
will pass to the new owner all those easements which are
necessary for the reasonable enjoyment of that part of the
property and which were used and enjoyed at the time of the
conveyance. If any reservations are to be made then they must
be expressly stated in the grant. The general maxim arising
from this being that a grantor shall not derogate from his grant.

Lyme Valley Squash Club Ltd v Newcastle under Lyme Borough Council and Another [1985] 2 All ER 405

This was an unusual case which raised questions about reservations for light in conveyances, and about implied easements
under section 62 of the Law of Property Act 1925. The squash
club purchased from the local council some land next to a car

park which also belonged to the council. It was agreed that there would be the usual reservations for the benefit of the council, that the club would not acquire rights over neighbouring land (the car park) and that the council would be free to develop upon it notwithstanding loss of light. Unfortunately this was omitted from the actual conveyance and trouble arose when the council wanted to build on the car park not long after the squash club had been built. Blackett-Ord V-C in the Chancery Division ruled that there was an implied easement in a conveyance giving the squash club a right to light and that they were entitled to financial damages. The sum of £10,000 was awarded. Upon reflection this would appear to be rather generous and difficult to justify under the normally accepted methods of valuing loss of light. If the council were somewhat unlucky, the lesson will have been learnt about drawing up similar conveyances in the future.

The second type of dispute can best be summed up in the words of Lord MacNaughton commenting on the fact that cases come to law often 'where the defendant has acted in a high-handed manner or where they have attempted to steal a march upon the plaintiff or to evade the jurisdiction of the Court'. Injunctions are usually the result and professional advisers should not condone such actions. One case which went to appeal should act as a lesson to all, namely, *Mathias v Davies* (1970) 214 EG 1111. Here an injunction was awarded to pull down an extension where the defendant had acted in a high-handed manner, building where he knew he was in the wrong.

The third type of case arises where in broad terms clarification of the Common Law is required and it is such cases which have given rise to the main body of case law on rights to light. There is a much-quoted phrase that it is better that the law be certain than right: on this particular topic it would be fair to say that the law has not yet reached a position of certainty. The words of Lord Lindley in *Colls* (see overleaf) still echo: 'There are elements of uncertainty which render it impossible to lay down any definite rule applicable to all cases.' With this proviso, some key cases will be outlined here in chronological order before the next chapter considers how the judgments have affected the arguments presented in rights to light disputes.

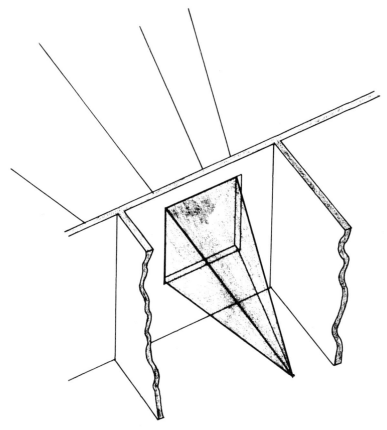

'Cone' of light entering through a window

Scott v Pape (1886) 31 ChD 554

This was an early case on the identity of light. The plaintiff
had redeveloped and built a larger building with more windows. There was some coincidence between the old and the
new windows but they were not entirely in the same position.
Cotton LJ and Bowen LJ both decided that the light which is
the subject of the right is a pencil or cone of light entering
through a defined window opening. Once the right is acquired
the window position can move and it is possible to transfer the
former rights by showing that the new windows still receive
some light from the cone or pencil of light which benefited the

original windows. The concept may be understood by thinking of a square window with the cone as a pyramid the point of which is in the room and the four sides of which extend out through the window frame to the sky beyond.

Shelfer v City of London Electric Lighting Co [1895] 1 Ch 287

Here the plaintiff sought an injunction against the Electric Lighting Company to prevent or restrain them from causing a nuisance by noise and vibration. Once it was established that there was a nuisance, matters focused on whether an injunction should be given or whether damages were an appropriate remedy. Kekewich J awarded damages but the Court of Appeal reversed the decision and granted an injunction. Lindley LJ stressed that damages should be awarded where the plaintiff has shown that he only wants money, or in vexatious and oppressive cases, or where the plaintiff has so conducted himself as to render it unjust to grant him more than pecuniary relief. A. L. Smith LJ suggested as a good working rule that damages rather than an injunction should be awarded with reference to four tests: Is the injury small? Is it capable of being estimated in financial terms? Is it adequately compensated by a small financial payment? Would it be oppressive to the defendant to grant an injunction? If the answers to all these are positive then damages are appropriate. These tests can be and are used in rights to light disputes.

Colls v Home & Colonial Stores [1904] AC 179

Reference has already been made to this case (see p. 9), and it is an essential case in determining the extent of any right to light. It clarified much of the uncertainty which had arisen following the Prescription Act 1832 and gave rise to the now-familiar phrase that the right acquired is to an amount of light sufficient for the ordinary notions of mankind. The judgment also gave further definition on the acquisition of a right to light with particular reference to section 3 of the Prescription Act

1832. Lord Lindley considered that in order to acquire a right to light there must be:

1. Access *and* use of light not just access alone (in this context access means the free passage of light over the servient tenement).
2. Access and use must be to, and for, some dwelling-house, workshop or other building.
3. Access and use must be actually enjoyed therewith.
4. Such enjoyment must be without interruption for twenty years.
5. If all the above are proved the right becomes absolute and indefeasible unless a deed or some writing is to the contrary.

Having established the guide-lines as to whether or not a right had been acquired, the judges went on to consider the extent of the right and concluded that the reduction of light must be substantial enough to render a house uncomfortable or, in the case of business premises, to prevent the injured party carrying on his business as beneficially as before. It is important to note that there is a difference between the light considered acceptable in residential buildings and that for business premises.

News of the World Ltd v Allen Fairhead & Sons Ltd [1931] 2 Ch 402

News of the World (NoW) rebuilt their premises so that some of the windows coincided to an extent with the former windows. When redevelopment was proposed for the building across the street shortly thereafter NoW claimed that this would infringe the areas of the new windows which were shown to have a part of the cone of light from the former windows. On the facts of the case, Farwell J held that since NoW had reduced their original ancient lights themselves they could not disregard the light which came through the whole of the new window, and accordingly there was no infringement. (However, he then slightly confused the overall situation by saying that it depended on whether one obstructed the cone of light for which one had – and still had – a right, to an extent where a nuisance would be caused.)

The idea of a pencil or cone of light, the ability to benefit from transferred rights and the quality or quantum of light have also been discussed in *Tapling v Jones* (1865) 20 CB (NS) 166; *Andrews v Waite* [1907] 2 Ch 500 and *Fishenden v Higgs and Hill Ltd* [1935] 153 LT 128. In this last case Lord Hanworth MR suggested in addition to comments on the above that the courts ought to incline against an injunction if possible whilst recognising in so doing that large value sites do give rise to large sums since it is all relative.

William Cory & Son Limited v City of London Real Property Company Limited (1954) 163 EG 514

This was a case in the High Court of Justice (Chancery Division) before Mr Justice Upjohn. It is held in high esteem because the method of determining what is reasonable in an objective form was upheld by the court. The case came before the judge when demolition of the defendant's original buildings had already started but before the new building was built, so specialists had to piece together the situation before and after. This was done by the use of Waldram diagrams, and an assessment of the light penetrating into the affected rooms. Upjohn J was prepared to accept the 50/50 rule as a 'very rough guide' as to which rooms were adequately lit, the argument being that if 50 per cent of the room still had a sky factor of 0.2 per cent then the daylight was satisfactory. The line under consideration, i.e. the average line of measurement beyond which the room is considered to have a poor level of light, has come to be known as the 'grumble line'. But it is important to stress that in practice the exercise considers the lighting to the room as a whole and there is no question of a room's being plunged into darkness beyond a certain point. On the facts of the case, it was held that the proposed building would cause an actionable nuisance. It was shown that the light to some of the affected rooms would be reduced to well within the 50/50 line taken from the windows, and as much less than 50 per cent of the room was adequately lit, an injunction was awarded. The decision was perhaps harsh on the developer as arguably it would have made little difference to the value of the neighbouring premises if the development as originally proposed had been allowed.

The case was also interesting in that it addressed and reiterated the position over partitioning which had been discussed by Lord Davey in *Colls*. The rights of the neighbouring owner are not affected by a change of use or rearrangement of the internal partitioning provided that it can be considered as being within the ordinary or reasonable purposes for the building in question and that it is not for some unusual purpose (e.g. making the room a photographic studio) or some other purpose requiring an unusual amount of light.

Ough v King [1967] 3 All ER 859

The *William Cory* case did much to bring certainty to the question of what was regarded as adequately lit or not. All was then well until 1967 when a decision of Glazebrook J in awarding damages to Mrs. Ough was upheld by the Court of Appeal. The bare facts were that in Gravesend there were two adjoining houses separated by a 6′ (approx 2 m) wide passage-way. Two windows serving the ground-floor room of Mrs. Ough's property had rights to light. The experts showed that the new extension on Mr. King's adjoining property resulted in an overall diminution of light by about one fifth but that at least half the room (50 per cent) remained adequately lit. The judge went to look at the property for himself and viewing it on a wintry February afternoon decided that it was dark. It was held that the 50/50 rule was not universal and regard must be had to the locality (a City of London office block as compared to a residential building in the provinces). The measure of damages was not limited to the capital sum required for the increased cost of lighting but rather to the difference in value to the house before and after the interference. Lord Denning, who was one of the appeal court judges, also suggested that the standards of light required by normal inhabitants are increasing.

Gamble v Doyle (1971) 219 EG 310

Undeterred, albeit slightly taken aback, the experts continued to use the 50/50 rule as an objective basis on which to assess rights to light claims. In this case the grumble line was accepted and, although the reduction in light was to a level well below the 50 per cent mark, damages only were awarded. It should be noted that this type of settlement reflects the way in which the vast majority of rights to light disputes are resolved.

Metaxides v Adamson (1971) 219 EG 935

If a building can obstruct light so can a wall, trellis or, for that matter, a tree. This is an aspect of the right to light question that has not yet been fully aired but should give rise to an interesting debate in the coming years. In this case the subject was touched upon as the dispute concerned a pyracantha and trelliswork with wisteria growing over it. The resultant obstruction caused a loss of light; it was held that this was sufficient to cause an actionable injury and damages were awarded.

Newham and Others v Lawson and Others [1971] 22 P & CR 852

This concerned a motion to seek an interlocutory injunction which was finally refused. Plowman J had to consider an obstruction affecting stained glass windows to a church. He doubted whether the church authorities who had a prescriptive right to light through the church windows were entitled to claim any greater degree of protection if those windows were stained glass rather than clear. The right is one for light through an aperture (window), but, on general, well-established principles, it is not a right to increase the burden on the servient tenement by, for example, darkening the glass. Following the ordinary notions dictum, it was held that the proposals did not affect the ordinary requirements of people attending the church.

Allen and Another v Greenwood and Another [1975] 1 All ER 819

This case set another precedent though it must be said that it appears to be unsupported by other decisions, not only on rights to light matters but also on the general position of easements. It concerned some neighbouring residential premises in Rochdale. The proposals for an extension to a property next door were objected to by neighbours as they would cause a loss of light to the neighbouring house and, more importantly, to a greenhouse situated in the back garden. The land on which the extension was proposed lay immediately to the south of the garden (and greenhouse) and in the ensuing period the

developer parked his caravan immediately alongside the greenhouse and erected a close-boarded fence. The result was a loss
of sunlight to the greenhouse and a lot of green tomatoes.

Half the greenhouse was considered by the court to be of
little use in terms of sunlight but nonetheless there was 'ample
light left . . . for everything except the special purpose of
growing certain plants'. Blackett-Ord V-C decided in the first
instance that this did not constitute a nuisance and dismissed
the case. The Court of Appeal allowed it and granted an injunction to preserve the sunlight. Goff LJ considered that you could
acquire by prescription a right to an exceptional amount of
light and that the injury was not only one of light but also of
loss of heat and other energising properties of the sun. Poten-
tially, this decision could have far-reaching effects as it has
generally been regarded that there is no right to sunlight. The
case also raised though without fully addressing it the question
of solar heating. How important this aspect becomes will
depend on the future popularity of this form of heating. It is
not hard to envisage immediately north of a development site
a building which has no windows facing onto it but which
does have solar panels. The outcome of a dispute could be most
interesting.

Pugh and Another v Howells and Another [1984] 48 P & CR 298

Another recent case to reach the Court of Appeal and to indicate
a tendency to protect existing rights and ensure that developers
respect them, particularly where residential properties are concerned. The defendant had a lean-to, which it was proposed to
demolish to build a new two-storey extension. The plaintiff
claimed that this would adversely affect the light to a kitchen
window and to one other ground-floor window of the neighbouring property. It would seem from the facts that the overall
loss of light was small and that in applying the 50/50 rule
sufficient light was shown to remain. However, the court
applied very strictly the four tests (see further below, p. 39)
from the *Shelfer* case – is the injury small, capable of being
estimated in financial terms, adequately compensated by a small
monetary payment, would it be oppressive to the defendant to
grant an injunction? – and considered that monetary compen-

sation was not sufficient. Whilst Francis J had initially awarded
£500 damages, the appeal judges overruled this and awarded a
mandatory injunction to remove the obstruction (i.e. take
down part of the new extension). What may in this instance
have swayed the decision was the action of the defendant who,
despite warnings, carried on building regardless, the obstruction (effectively the top storey of the new two-storey extension)
being mainly constructed over a bank holiday week-end.
Applying a view that was also stated in the *Shelfer* case, the
court considered that an injunction was appropriate where a
defendant hurried up his building works to avoid an injunction
or acted with a reckless disregard for the plaintiff's rights, such
as proceeding after warnings. The principle is that one person
cannot buy off another person's rights.

Carr Saunders v Dick McNeil Associates Ltd and Others [1986] 1 WLR 922

As if to redress the balance, a note of optimism and some
certainty comes from this last case which concerned buildings
of commercial use in the Covent Garden area of London.
Despite the arguments put forward by the consultant for the
defendant it was clear that there was a loss of light, that this left
less than 50 per cent and that there was a justifiable actionable
nuisance. The good news for consultants and advisers was that
the 50/50 rule was followed (though only to the extent that it
is a useful guide), that the normally agreed methods of valuing
loss of light were accepted and that once again it was confirmed
that reflected light should not be taken into account. The not
such good news for developers was that the judge awarded
parasitic damages, i.e. damages not only for the injury that
was actionable but also for other matters or injuries which on
their own would not have been actionable. The result in this
instance was to multiply the loss of light damages figure by
approximately three. The judge also considered the effect of
partitioning, a relevant question when looking at open-plan
offices and the increasing use of demountable partitioning. Reference should also be made in particular to *Price v Hilditch*
[1930] 1 Ch 500, on partitioning and on the question of the use
to which the injured property has been put.

This chapter looks at the typical rights to light disputes that arise and the arguments and evidence used to settle them. All disputes have as their origin the desire of one party to protect his rights to his premises. This most often takes the form of resisting or objecting to some development on some neighbouring land. Alternatively, it may mean one owner's taking steps to protect his or her land and these being in turn resisted by a neighbour who sees them as detrimental to his rights in the future. An example of the latter is the registering of a notional screen (see further below, pp. 41–2).

The type of dispute will depend upon the level or the extent to which it is pursued. At the lowest level it may go no further than a discussion over the garden fence and possible retaliatory action such as inconsiderate use of the lawn mower early one Sunday morning. At the other extreme, funds and patience permitting, it may end up at the House of Lords, with subsequent heartache and misery on one side or the other, or even both. A prime rule is, whenever possible, to try to avoid legal proceedings.

In any potential dispute the facts need to be ascertained. A developer should consult with a designer in order to appreciate the likely risk at an early stage. Similarly an adjoining owner should investigate the position early on and try to avoid taking up a case once the obstruction is actually in place. The chances of being able to protect any rights are reduced once the new building or obstruction is in position. An adjoining owner should also think carefully before embarking on a course of objection. It may be that a development on some neighbouring land whilst affecting the rights to light of a property may actually improve the value of the land or improve the chance of being able to undertake similar development works.

Where a dispute has arisen, and the respective parties have taken legal advice or consulted an expert (or usually both), what arguments could be used in determining whether this were a valid claim and if it were what might be required to pursue and prove the claim? The extent to which any of the items below are material will depend upon the facts of the individual case but these examples should give some insight into the subject.

Grounds for Argument

Fundamentally, there are two opposing aims. On the one hand the dominant tenement (usually the plaintiff or neighbouring owner) has to show that he has acquired a right and that the proposed building will infringe this. On the other hand the servient tenement (usually the defendant or developer) has to show that any infringement is either non-actionable or, more often than not, if it is actionable, that a reasonable monetary settlement is a suitable remedy.

Chapter 2 considered the easement of light and how it is acquired. If there is a written agreement the document will need to be interpreted and the proposals examined in the context of it. This is, more often than not, a factual exercise upon which the respective consultants can agree. If the document is *prohibitive* (see pp. 6–7) then any proposed breach will require re-negotiation of the terms. If it is *permissive* common law principles will usually apply and consideration should be given to such matters as the 50/50 rule and the four following tests which have already been referred to (see above, the *Shelfer* case, pp. 31 and 36), all of which can give rise to much argument in themselves.

Is the injury small?   The word small is subjective. If a building has very good or more than ample natural light it is possible to lose a large amount of this and still not suffer too badly. Conversely, the existing light may be very poor and in such a case even a tiny loss may give rise to a large problem, as there is none to spare.

Is it capable of being estimated in financial terms?   A much-quoted example is that of the Rose window of York Minster. A developer might perhaps argue that a contribution to the restoration fund would be suitable recompense.

Is it adequately compensated by a small financial payment?   A cynic may say that every person has their price and, as noted above, 'small' is subjective. However, most residential neighbouring owners simply want to stop the development going ahead.

Would it be oppressive to the defendant to grant an injunction?   Consideration would be given to the actions of the parties, the type of properties involved and their location. In the *Cory* case (see above, p. 33) the judge considered that a major property company would not be too inconvenienced if it were not able to maximise one out of a large portfolio of properties.

Abandonment of the Right to Light

If a right has been acquired or is claimed, a developer may seek to argue that in fact the right has been abandoned or what is claimed has not been acquired. It has been held that there must be an intention permanently to abandon the right and that non-use does not diminish the right. For example, a right will not be lost automatically if the building is demolished (see *Ecclesiastical Commissioners for England v Kino* [1880] 14 ChD 213). The arguments over transferred rights are applicable here and, before any technical exercises are undertaken, the old and new building need to be considered in general terms. Does the new building continue to use in access terms the light which it formerly enjoyed and is that use substantially identical? For example, there would be a strong case for transferred rights if a building were demolished and rebuilt behind a retained façade notwithstanding a change of use.

An argument can be made for interruption giving rise to an effective abandonment of a right. This can be caused by the dominant tenement bricking up a window opening or by the servient tenement erecting a screen (providing this is done without objection). There must be 'some unequivocal act of intentional abandonment' – Lord Chelmsford in *Tapling v Jones* (1865) 20 CB (NS) 166. A pile of boxes stacked up against a window or some heavy curtaining, whilst effectively blocking out the light within the dominant tenement, has been held not to be an abandonment of the right. There must however be a clearly defined aperture intended 'for the admission of light' – *Presland v Bingham* [1889] 41 ChD 268. The aperture need not necessarily be glazed (in some cases, e.g. castles, they may not be), but it is unlikely that the presence of a doorway would be sufficient unless, perhaps, the door was partly glazed, as in a back-door to a kitchen.

Abandonment can be shown if there is a licence or deed. For example, if owner A gives permission to neighbour B to build a wall which clearly infringes A's light then there is a presumption that A would have abandoned any former rights at least to the extent of the obstruction.

One of the characteristics of an easement is that a landowner cannot acquire a right over his own land. Thus if at any time the dominant and the servient tenement, i.e. the two properties which respectively benefit from and are subject to an easement, are in the same hands, in other words, there was unity of seisin or title, such a period would usually be ignored in settling a dispute concerning an easement.

The Lost Modern Grant

A further point to consider here is the question of a 'lost grant'. The Prescription Act 1832 (section 4) says that the period of time in which the easement was enjoyed should be taken as the period 'next before some suit or action', i.e. leading up to and immediately before the legal action that is to resolve the dispute. What happens, however, if the dominant tenement 'lost' a part of that preceding period (because, for example, the servient tenement had been lately sold to the Crown, and there is no right to light over Crown Land)? It is possible that a landowner in such a case could rely on the concept of the lost 'modern grant': a legal doctrine, surviving from before the Prescription Act, that the court can assume that a grant existed for some time prior to its recent loss. The doctrine of the lost modern grant is governed by the Limitation Act 1980, which gives up to six years after the injury in which to claim.

Notional Screens or Light Obstruction Notices

Historically, if an owner wanted to prevent a neighbour acquiring a right to light over his land, he had to reach an agreement with the neighbour or else physically block out the light. This would often have been done by means of corrugated iron screens supported by timber framing or scaffolding. Following the large-scale destruction of the Second World War and the Town and Country Planning Act 1947, it was realised that bomb sites might be blighted as a result of neighbouring buildings acquiring additional rights over them. Since it was no longer permissible to erect eighty-foot-high scaffold screening structures at will the concept of a notional screen was developed and subsequently incorporated in the Rights of Light Act 1959.

Section 1 of this Act dealt with temporary provisions and extended the prescription period by seven years in certain cases. However, section 1 was subsequently repealed by the Statute Law (Repeals) Act 1974 and the prescription period remains a uniform twenty years under the Prescription Act 1832. Sections 2 and 3 of the 1959 Act were permanent measures but were amended by section 17 of the Local Land Charges Act 1975. These sections enable an owner of land to register a notional screen for the benefit of his land. This is taken to be an opaque structure of a height stated and in the position shown on the application. It is usually effective for one year which – in the context of section 4 of the 1832 Act (see above, p. 8) – is sufficient to prevent a neighbouring owner acquiring or continuing to have a right to light. The light obstruction notice can be cancelled before the year is up and, in an emergency, a temporary notice – issued under section 2(3)(b) – can be registered, but these usually expire within the year.

The owner of the neighbouring land (the dominant tenement) has a right of action and can object to the notice, for example, if he considers that he has already acquired a right to light and that the notional screen would obstruct this (see section 2, ss.(3), (4), (5) and (6)). Section 4 of the Act preserves the immunity of the Crown although it is possible to register a notice which has the effect of preventing the Crown acquiring rights over the land which is the subject of the notice. As with the Prescription Act, the 1959 Act does not apply to Scotland.

It should be noted that a notice lasts for a maximum period of one year, at the end of which the prescriptive clock is turned back to zero. Therefore the notice must be re-registered at least every nineteen years to prevent the dominant tenement obtaining its right to light after twenty uninterrupted years.

When a registration is being considered, the Lands Tribunal Rules 1975 (SI 1975/299) and the Local Land Charges Rules 1977 (SI 1977/985) and subsequent amendments thereof need to be consulted.

Layout of Dominant Tenement

Another point which may be at issue relates to the layout of and use within the dominant tenement. There has been in recent years, in the City of London in particular, a large demand for enormous open-plan clear space floors for financial dealing purposes. This means if natural light is required at all for these floors, which is arguable, much better angles of sky visibility are needed to enable natural light to penetrate anywhere other than near the windows. At the other extreme, an office block subdivided by partitioning into small cellular units, each with a window, could lose considerable light and still have at least 50 per cent of each shallow office unit adequately lit. In the *Carr-Saunders* case (see above, p. 37), where a materially different answer was arrived at if the offices were partitioned, the judge concluded that the right to light is measured in terms not only of the particular use to which the dominant tenement has been put in the past but also of the potential uses to which it could be put in the future. (See also *Moore v Hall* (1878) 3 QBD 178; *Price v Hilditch* [1930] 1 Ch 500 and *Sheffield Masonic Hall Co. v Sheffield Corporation* [1932] 2 Ch 17.)

The evidence required to settle a dispute comes from two main sources. The first relates to the question of whether a right exists notwithstanding the nature of the obstruction. This, as we have seen, necessitates examining the rights of the respective parties – age and nature of the premises, agreements, notional screens and actions that have been taken leading up to the hearing. The second relates to the actual obstruction and injury. The method of assessing and compensating for these is discussed in the next chapter.

Two ways of introducing more light into a property or of accommodating rights to light requirements

Valuing the Right to Light

As with any legal matter, the decision whether to defend one's right to light or one's right to obstruct someone else's light has to be taken on whether the benefits that could accrue and the costs which may be borne will be worth it. To understand the factors to be taken into account the value that can be attributed to the right to light needs to be appreciated. On a large commercial project, the calculation for the developer is fairly simple. Value can be measured in terms of area. The larger the area of the building the larger the rent received. Once the costs of buying the land, constructing the building and financing it are subtracted, what is left is the profit. It is not difficult to envisage a situation where a developer is prepared to infringe the light to neighbouring properties in anticipation of being able to settle claims for loss of light at reasonably acceptable levels of financial compensation. In many situations all parties are happy with this; sometimes the neighbour can take the opportunity to make provisions for future development of his own site by entering into a reciprocal agreement.

It is, however, more difficult when financial compensation is neither appropriate nor acceptable to the injured party. The courts do not encourage a view whereby you can buy someone's rights to light. Lord Sumner (in *Leeds Industrial Co-Operative Society Ltd v Slack* [1924] AC 851) stated that the '. . . jurisdiction to give damages where it exists is not so to be used as in fact to enable the defendant to purchase from the plaintiff against his will his legal right to the easement.' That is not to say that the courts will not award damages but rather to emphasise their discretionary nature.

On a project of a domestic nature, it is unlikely that the owner building an extension has sufficient cash to pay the neighbour for infringing his light and it is even more unlikely that the neighbour would consider a cash payment a suitable reimbursement for the light lost.

Where financial damages are an appropriate remedy the basis on which they are calculated is as follows. A specialist assesses initially the actual loss of light by the use of illustrative means such as Waldram diagrams. A weighting is then given according to where in the room in question the light will actually be reduced. The light nearer the window tends to be more valuable since the light usually diminishes the further into the room you go. It is possible to lose a good deal of light from the back of a room and still have sufficient in the remainder. A calculation based on the rental value multiplied by a percentage which reflects the proportion of the rent regarded as attributable to the natural light available (a room with no natural light will have a lower rental per square foot than a room with windows allowing light in) is then made. The total sum is then capitalised effectively to give a value based on a freeholder in possession. As it is possible for lessees as well as freeholders to have the benefit of rights, the sum can be subdivided to reflect the reversionary nature of the interest.

In the case of domestic properties, the principles above are equally applicable but the courts have in the past looked to surveyors to provide a valuation based on the difference in the value of a house before and after the loss of light. It is not considered sufficient merely to value the extra cost of the electricity bill over a period of time.

The value of the loss of light is therefore based on the loss to the injured party rather than on the gain to the defendant. In certain situations, usually commercial, the gain can be substantial and, consequently, the courts, in order to modify the benefits, may award parasitic damages to take into account not only the loss of light but also the general loss of amenity that has arisen. The damages are fixed at the time that the injury takes place with a capital sum exchanging hands immediately. In a period of rising capital values for property this can be advantageous to the developer. The loss to the neighbour is a permanent one whilst the extra space gained by the developer will increase in value.

Where the infringement is large the position of the neighbouring owner is strengthened. In such situations, a developer can often be persuaded to pay a slightly larger sum in financial compensation in order to settle a claim and both parties may find this acceptable. If there is a covenant of a prohibitive nature which the developer is seeking to violate then the neighbouring owner's position is stronger still. However, should avarice be apparent on the part of the neighbour, then the developer can consider requesting the Lands Tribunal (under s. 84 of the Law of Property Act 1925) to set the covenant aside or modify it. It is worth noting that a restrictive covenant is not a right to light agreement, although it is often loosely referred to as such when it is concerned with daylighting matters. It may restrict building on neighbouring land and incidentally, but quite adequately, prevent obstruction of light. Where the Lands Tribunal is asked to set aside or modify a covenant, it tends to ignore the 'blackmail value' which is conferred by the existence of a covenant. The courts will not condone behaviour that they regard as extortionate and there is a tendency for such incidents to rebound on the greedy neighbour. In the commercial property world bad news travels fast, and in the long term there is little to be gained.

There is no market in rights to light. Once a claim is made and settled that is the end of the matter: should a neighbour acquire a property whilst the building next door is being constructed he will have no additional claim for loss of light if the vendor has already settled a claim with the developer. Although, in theory, a developer could acquire a neighbour's right to light over his land, by means of a written agreement, years in advance of a development, in practice it is rarely done as it is usually of more benefit to both parties to leave any negotiation until the point where the infringement is in the process of taking place. Whilst not strictly rights to light, in North America air rights can be sold and in areas of commercial use there is seemingly little to prevent a developer infringing the light to neighbouring office blocks. In recent years, air space over railway stations in central London has been sold to developers but this does not diminish the rights of neighbouring owners to object to the loss of light from the ensuing development.

Avoidance of Legal Proceedings

Very few rights to light claims result in a court case. Invariably, experts are appointed and the matter is settled. However, all the experts must eventually depend on their clients agreeing to a suggested settlement.

When an infringement of a right to light is imminent or has taken place the injured party's only remedy is an injunction. In simple terms, this can be either in a *quia timet* or an interlocutory action according to whether or not the infringement has already taken place. If an interlocutory injunction is obtained, then it is probable that the neighbour will be asked to give an undertaking that he will pay the costs of any delay to the developer if he is unsuccessful at trial. The injunction will be either an order to restrain the development from going ahead in its present form or a mandatory one requiring demolition of the obstruction that has been constructed. But before embarking on legal proceedings, a neighbour should try to negotiate with the developer, and the solicitor should advise on some form of discourse before committing either party to the high costs of a lawsuit. On a large commercial project, the costs of delaying the development can run into many thousands of pounds a week. At the other end of the scale, diplomatic relations with the next-door neighbour building an extension are almost certain to be broken off if a writ is issued to stop the extension.

Before issuing a writ the neighbour should obtain even on a preliminary basis the opinion of a specialist in rights to light matters to establish the legal position, to estimate quickly the magnitude of any claim and, most important, to give an objective assessment. He must distinguish between direct light (for which there is an easement) and indirect or reflected light (for which there is not). He must counteract the difficulty of recollecting and comparing the light previously enjoyed with that now available, clouded as the injured party's memory may be by a feeling of a loss of privacy and a spoilt view. However, although the professional may be able to measure amounts of light with scientific detachment, it has been argued that expert evidence as to the quantity of light which can be expected is not as good as that of those actually using the room in question. None the less whilst having regard for the locality in the context of what can be considered as reasonable development, he has to avoid making judgements based on such subjective matters as view and outlook.

It is worth noting *CEMP Properties (UK) Ltd v Dentsply Research and Development Corporation.* (EG, September 1989), in which the solicitor's failure to make known to the purchaser the existence of deeds concerning a neighbour's right to light over the premises resulted in the purchaser's redevelopment having to be redesigned. While the court here was particularly concerned with assessing appropriate damages, the case is a reminder that easements are ignored at everybody's peril.

Planning Permission and the Right to Light

It must be emphasised that the granting of planning permission does not affect a legal right to light. The considerations taken into account are for the most part different. However, the majority of developments that give rise to rights to light disputes have required planning permission in the first place. An understanding of the factors involved in the planning process is therefore important both for the developer who, having obtained planning permission for a scheme, does not wish to see it frustrated by a neighbouring owner and for the neighbour, who has no legal right to light, for whom the planning process may be the only opportunity to influence the design of a proposed development.

It is perhaps regrettable that there is not more uniformity between the factors taken into account in designing for light to satisfy common law rights to light and planning requirements. It is not only the layman who is puzzled by some of the decisions. Every specialist undoubtedly has a number of examples of schemes having been refused planning consent on daylighting grounds although a study has shown there to be no material loss of light. Equally, consent for other schemes has been granted with seemingly little regard for the catastrophic loss of light that will result to neighbouring buildings. As each planning authority has differing priorities so the importance of planning for light will vary.

A developer and, in turn, the chosen designer has to try to establish the level of priority that the planning authority is likely to give to daylighting, usually through consultation with the planning officer. In a residential area there tends to be greater concern for the amenities of nearby residents. In a depressed derelict area the overall need for constructive development may outweigh the possible detrimental effect to a few.

In the early 1970s the Department of the Environment Welsh Office published a study entitled 'Sunlight and Daylight – Planning Criteria and Design of Buildings' (HMSO, 1972). This put forward suggested criteria to assist both planning authorities and developers to provide for sunlight and daylight in the layout and design of buildings. This document has been widely used and in many cases provides a helpful starting-point. Daylight and sunlight protractors are explained and these are valuable when considering basic massing of a scheme.

It soon becomes apparent that a tall thin building such as a tower block may more easily provide for adequate daylight to neighbouring buildings, as light can pass by the sides of it, than a lower wider building where daylight is restricted to the amount that can effectively pass over the top of it. The building designer needs to consider the question of light in both plan and section. In early rights to light disputes the 45° rule was often quoted and relied upon: it was felt that a proposed building would not interfere with the light to a neighbouring building if it did not extend past a notional 45° line extended up from the sill of the neighbouring building's ground-floor window. This is no longer regarded as satisfactory from a rights to light point of view as compliance with a single factor in isolation is often inappropriate.

If a consensus of opinion is reached between the planning officer and developer and permission is subsequently granted, then attention can be focused more on the legal position of the neighbouring owner. It is not unknown, however, for a recommendation from the planning officer to be rejected by the planning committee on daylighting grounds. In such instances an appeal should be made, based on objective daylighting criteria. It seems inappropriate that, with accepted objective methods of measuring light, an application can still fail on the subjective views of a committee.

Where an application becomes the subject of a planning inquiry, any arguments over daylight and sunlight should be referred to a specialist. The use of diagrams and, in particular, models are particularly helpful in visualising the impact of a scheme. It is for example possible to work out from these how

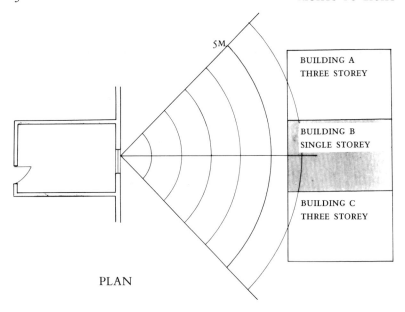

PLAN

RESIDENTIAL BUILDING TO BUILDING

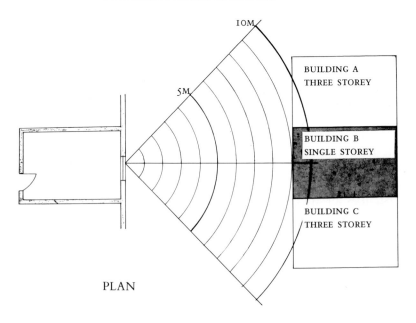

PLAN

NON-RESIDENTIAL BUILDING TO BUILDING

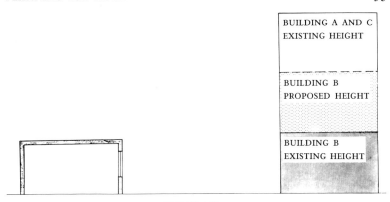

| BUILDING A AND C EXISTING HEIGHT |
| BUILDING B PROPOSED HEIGHT |
| BUILDING B EXISTING HEIGHT |

SECTION

Daylight indicator   The appropriate daylight indicator is based on the plan either on the face of the building or on the boundary. There are different indicators for residential and non-residential buildings. The heights marked on the arcs of the indicators are relative to a datum point taken 2m above the actual ground level whatever height that may be. They provide an answer of reasonable accuracy as to whether or not buildings satisfy the appropriate block spacing criterion, i.e. achieve the sky component specified therein. Depending on the indicator used, a permissible height for the development can be established or, alternatively, it can be proved that there will be sufficient light passing round the sides of the development to satisfy the daylight criterion. There are also indicators for sunlight.

much direct sunlight will fall on a terrace or garden at different times of the year with and without the proposed obstruction.

The position of the designer is one of balancing the wishes of a client with those of the planning authority. The designer should not forget that, whatever the stance of the planners, the rights to light question usually remains unconsidered. It is therefore prudent to propose massing the structure in such a way as to mitigate as far as possible the likely areas of conflict. The designer should look at the surrounding buildings and note where the windows are, and their relationship with the subject site. He or she should draw up representative sections and mark on the existing angles of light. Mansards or set-backs may be needed at upper levels. Where windows are close to the boundary it may be necessary to provide light-wells on the site to maintain adequate light. At the same time, the designer should take advantage of blank walls on the neighbouring site.

The current Building Regulations have provisions concerning windows (openings) on or adjacent to the boundary of a site. If the design requires these it may be necessary to seek a relaxation of the Regulations. The Building Control Officer (District Surveyor) may require evidence that an agreement has been reached with the neighbouring owner since such windows could have implications for the extent of future development on the adjacent site.

Scope for Infringement of Light

If a neighbouring development is new (and as such unlikely to have any rights to light), there is scope for a substantial infringement of light. Planning consultation is nevertheless important as the authority may still seek to protect the daylight on general amenity grounds; but the planning authority can for example take into account a profile agreement between neighbours allowing an infringement of light to take place.

The developer is usually keen to maximise the size of a development be it a residential extension or an office block. It is virtually impossible, particularly in a city centre, not to alter the angles of light to neighbouring buildings when increasing the shape and size (mass) of the building envelope. If the developer does not realise this, the designer should draw attention to it. The developer must then decide on the design strategy. Where the risks of infringement seem to be too great, there is merit in changing the design during the planning stage. Should a rights to light claim be successful, not only could the design need altering, but it may be necessary to go back and make a new planning application.

If necessary, the designer or the developer should call in a specialist during the early design stage prior to applying for planning permission, to highlight the particularly sensitive areas. There are two approaches: either the preferred scheme can be designed and then commented upon in terms of its infringement on neighbouring buildings; or the specialist can provide a set of guide-lines, within which it is unlikely that there will be any actionable infringement, and the design can be drawn up accordingly. Of these, the first is usually preferred as the latter can often result in too much compromise at an early stage. However, it is once planning permission has been obtained that the rights to light issue is invariably raised.

BIBLIOGRAPHY

Nicholson Combe, R. G., *Law of Light*, Butterworth & Co., 1911.

DSIR Illumination Research Technical Paper No. 7, 'The Penetration of Daylight and Sunlight into Buildings', HMSO, 1932.

DSIR Illumination Research Technical Paper No. 17, 'Seasonal Variation of Daylight Illumination', HMSO, 1932.

Waldram, Percy J., *A Measuring Diagram for Daylight Illumination*, B. T. Batsford, 1950.

Walsh, J. W. T., *The Science of Daylight*, MacDonald, London, 1961.

Anstey, B., and Chavasse, M., *The Right to Light*, Estates Gazette Limited, 1963.

Hopkinson, R. G., Petherbridge, P., Longmore, J., *Daylighting*, Heinemann, 1966.

'Sunlight and daylight – planning criteria and design of buildings', Dept of the Environment Welsh Office, HMSO, 1972.

Jackson, P., *The Law of Easements and Profits*, Butterworth & Co., 1978.

BSI Drafts for Development DD67 and DD73: 'Basic design for the design of buildings: sunlight', 1980; 'Daylight', 1982.

BS 8206: Lighting for buildings, BSI, 1985.

BRE Digests 309 and 310, Building Research Establishment, Dept of the Environment, 1986.

Maurice, Spencer G., *Gale on Easements*, 15th ed., Sweet & Maxwell, 1986.

Halsbury's Laws of England, 4th ed., completed 1988.

INDEX

abandonment 40–1
access 40
  business premises 32
agreements 6, 7
  checking title 17
  existing: developer and 13
    purchaser and 12
  permissive 6, 8
  prohibitive 6, 8
  renegotiating 13
air rights 47
amenities, protection of rights
  50, 54
'Ancient Lights' 2, 9
artificial light 20, 22–3
atria 13

bomb sites, blighted 42
Building Control Officer 53
building materials:
  cladding 14, 16
  reflectiveness 22
  see also light-wells
Building Regulations:
  meeting requirements of 15
  relaxation of 53
Building Research
  Establishment:
  correction factors for
    percentage reductions 22
  light-measuring methods 21

Charges Register 12
CIE standard overcast sky 21
compensation 31
  anticipating acceptable 45

for domestic infringements
  45–6
insufficient 36–7
test for 31, 36, 40
construction, control of 2
covenants, restrictive:
  designer and 15
  on land use 12
  violation of 47
Crown Land immunity 10–11,
  42
  and lost grant 41

damages 39
  assessing 29, 34, 37
  avarice over 47
  basis for calculating 46
  'blackmail value' 47
  court attitude to 45
  parasitic 37, 46
  test for 31, 36, 39–40
daylight:
  assessing for inquiry 51–2
  average minimum
    requirement 25
  components 20
  correction factors for
    percentage reduction 22
  planning standards 2, 51
  rejection of plans over 51–2
  variations in 23
daylight indicator 52
daylight plans 19
daylight protractors 21, 51
daylight table 21
deeds, abandonment and 41

demolition 40
  of extensions 13, 29
  injunctions after 33–4
  mandatory order for 48
designer:
  and daylighting 50–1
  problems for 15–16
  and reflected components 22
  and risk of light
    infringement 54
  use of plans/sections 51, 53
developer:
  and daylighting 50–1
  and design strategy 54
  evasion of court jurisdiction
    29
  and planning process 50
  problems for 13–15
development:
  effect of size 54
  notice of 17
  order restraining 48
  planning objections to 17
  valuing site 45
diagrams 51–3
direct light, assessing for court
    action 48
disputes:
  after completion 38
  appreciating risk of 38
  artificial light in 23
  easements in 39
  grounds for argument 39–40
  origin of 38
  over conveyances 28–9
  paying delay costs 17–18, 48
  settling 18, 38ff.
  sky component in 23
  sources of evidence 43
  specialist opinions 48–9
  tests applied in 31, 36–7,
    39–40
  types of 28–30
  under Common Law 29

  unresolved 13
  variables in 20
  see also Waldram diagrams
dominant tenant:
  and abandonment of right 40
  aim in dispute 39
  layout and use 43
  rights 5
    of vacant 5–6
  and temporary notice 42
doors, part-glazed 41
double glazing correction
    factor 22
dwelling-house:
  access of light to 32
  calculating damages for 46
  increasing light standards 34
  rights; of new 17
    under Acts 8, 9

easements 5ff., 18
  documented; comparing
    with obstruction 23, 25
    interpretation in dispute 39
  dominant land 5
  implied 29
  over own land 6
  permissive 39
  precedent on general
    position 35–6
  prohibitive 39
  time enjoyed 41
  transfer for buildings 6
  under Common Law 8–9
  and unity of seisin 41
  see also lost modern grant
extensions 13, 17, 29, 34, 35–6
  replacing 36–7

façade, retained 40
field 6
50/50 rule 10, 33, 34, 37
  application of 36–7
  consideration of locality 34
  in disputes 39

45° rule 51
freeholder, acquiring rights 2
  see also landlords

garden 6, 35–6
glass blocks, correction factors
  22
glazing, allowing for 21
glazing bars, correction factors
  22
grant of light 6
grant, lost modern 41
greenhouse, loss of light to
  35–6
'grumble line' 10, 33
  acceptance of 34

injunctions 31, 33–4
  after demolition 33–4
  avoidance of 37
  granting 29
  interlocutory 48
  on large-value sites 18, 33
  to remove obstruction 36–7
  test for 31, 36, 40
injuries, actionable 35, 37
  assessing 10
  test for 31, 36, 39
interference, actionable 10
International Commission on
  Illumination see CIE
interruption, and abandonment
  40

land rights see dominant land;
  servient land
landlords:
  developing adjacent land 18
  informing of developments
    18
  and lost 'modern grant' 41
  rights over own land 41
  severe restrictions on 4
Lands Tribunal 12, 47
Lands Tribunal Rules 1975 43

latitude, effect on sunlight 23
Law of Property Act 1925:
  section 62 28
  section 84 47
leaseholders, rights 18, 46
legal proceedings, avoidance of
  48–9
  issuing writ 48
licence:
  abandonment and 41
  on windows 12
light 1–2, 18
  assessing residue 10
  definition of sufficient 10, 31
    see also 50/50 rule
  designing for 13, 50
  identity of 30–1
  infringement of 54
  introducing more 44
  loss of: assessing 32, 37, 46
    defining 10
    valuing 29
  for replacement building 40
  reservation of 6
  see also artificial light;
    daylight; sunlight
light, rights to:
  absolute 9
    and future development 2
    proving 32
  accommodating
    requirements 44
  acquiring 4, 6–8
    guide-lines for 32
    years before development
      47
  assessments 22
  buying 45
  over Crown land 10–11
  definition of 5–6
  express creation 6
  guide-lines for measuring 25
  implied 6
  protecting existing 36–7

proving 4, 43
twenty-year period 8, 32
  adjustments to 9
valuing 45–7
see also abandonment;
  disputes; planning
  permission; prescription
light obstruction notice 41–2
light 'cone' 30–1
  and transferred rights 32–3
light meters 27
light-wells 13, 53
  cladding for 14, 16
  set-backs in 3
Limitation Act 1980 41
Local Land Charges Act 1975,
  section 17 42
Local Land Charges Rules 1977
  43
lost modern grant 41
lumens:
  definition of 27
  whole sky advantages 26
    summer 27
    winter 25, 27

mansards 16, 53
models/mock-ups 19, 51–3

natural features, and sunlight
  23
negotiation, before legal
  proceedings 48
neighbours:
  cash payments to 45–6
  and development: no
    obligation to inform 15
    obstructing 16–17
    paying costs of delay
      17–18, 48
  establishing legal position 48
  imposing severe limitations
    on 4
  maintenance of natural light
    13–15

and planning process 50, 51
  inspection of applications
    17
  problems for 16–18
  profile agreement between
    54
  reciprocal agreements 45
  specific rights over 5
  unresolved disputes with 13
notional screen 18, 41–2
  extension of period 42
  registering 38
nuisance, actionable 35–6
  assessing after demolition
    33–4
  obstruction as 10
  use of noise/vibration tests 31

obstruction:
  claims for 8
  defining 10
  fire escapes as 16
  and loss of light 8
  plant room as 16
  see also light obstruction
    notices; nuisance
offices 9
  open-plan 43
  see also partitions
ordinary notions dictum 35
orientation, and sunlight 23
outlook, protecting 16
overshadowing 23

partitioning, internal 33–4, 37,
  43
planning application:
  considerations: and derelict
    areas 50–1
    and residential areas 50
  rejection of 51
  successful claim and 54
  unresolved 13
planning authorities 50

planning inquiry, advice on
    51–3
planning permission:
    and owner's right to light 2,
    50ff.
planning process:
    guide-lines within 2
    understanding 50
prescription 8–9
    extensions of period 42
    right to light and heat 36
Prescription Act 1832:
    and blighted land 9
    immunity of the Crown
    10–11
    section 3 8–9, 10, 31–2
    section four 8, 41, 42
    time limit 42
privacy, protecting 16
purchaser, problems for 12–13

reflected light 6
    assessments and 22
        before legal proceedings
        48
    external 20, 22
    internal 20, 22
    in judgments 37
rental value, when calculating
    loss of light 46
Rights of Light Act 1959 9
    sections 1, 2 42
    section 3 9, 42

screen, erection of 40
    corrugated iron 41–2
    high scaffolding 42
seasons, and sunlight 23
servient tenement:
    and abandonment of rights
    40
    aim in dispute 39
    in easement context 5
    see also neighbours
set-backs 3, 13, 14, 16, 53

shadow-path, measuring 23
shadows 23
shops, rights 9
sky, standard overcast 21
sky component 20, 21
    in disputes 23
    see also Waldram diagrams
sky factor:
    calculating 27
    contours 25
solar heating 36
solicitor, problems for 18
space, between buildings 8
    application of 50/50 rule 34
    planning standards 2
Statute Law (Repeals) Act 1974
    42
sunlight 6, 20
    assessing for inquiry 51–3
    clouding of 23
    definition of 23
    in disputes 23
    planning and: criteria 51
        standards 2
'Sunlight and Daylight –
    Planning Criteria and
    Design of Buildings' (DoE)
    51
sunlight plans 19
sunlight protractors 51
sun-path, measuring 23
surveyor:
    problems for 19
    site inspection by 19
        hired by neighbours for 17
    technical analysis 19
    valuing lost light 46

table height, in light assessment
    25
temporary notices 42–3
tenants, and neighbouring
    development 18

tenement *see* dominant
  tenement; servient tenement
tower blocks 51
town and country planning
  system 2
transferred rights 30–1, 32–3
  and abandonment 40
  see also windows
trees 35
trelliswork 35

view, right to 6

Waldram, Percy J. 23–5
Waldram diagrams 21, 23–7
  for assessments: of damages
  46
  after demolition 33–4
  section/plan 24
walls:
  abandonment and 41
  blank 6

use of neighbouring 53
  garden 35
warehouse, rights 9
window frames:
  allowing for 21
  correction factors 22
windows:
  blocking up 12
  abandonment and 40
  external obstructions to 40
  on or adjacent to boundary
  12
  allowances for 53
  Building Regulations and
  16
  on opposite side of street 16
  shed 28
  stained glass 35
  transfer of rights 30–1, 32–3
  unglazed 40–1
workshop, rights:
  of access of light 32
  under Prescription Act 8